BEST-LOVED

IRISH

BALLADS

First published in hardback 2020 by The O'Brien Press Ltd,
12 Terenure Road East, Rathgar, Dublin 6, D06 HD27, Ireland.
Tel: +353 1 4923333; Fax: +353 1 4922777
E-mail: books@obrien.ie
Website: www.obrien.ie
The O'Brien Press is a member of Publishing Ireland.

ISBN: 978-1-78849-220-1
Cover design: Emma Byrne

Images courtesy of Shutterstock: pages 8, 16, 20, 24, 30, 36, 40, 44,
46, 52, 56, 60, 64, 68, 72, 74, 78, 82, 86, 94, 100, 104, 106, 110, 114,
118, 122, 126, 130, 132, 136, 140, 144, 148, 152, 158; Wikimedia
Commons/Herbert Ortner: page 10; Alamy: page 90

10 9 8 7 6 5 4 3 2 1
25 24 23 22 21 20

Printed and bound in Poland by Białostockie Zakłady Graficzne S.A.
The paper in this book is produced using pulp from managed forests.

Thanks to Paul Brady for allowing us to use and adapt his version of
'Arthur McBride'.

Published in:

BEST-LOVED

IRISH

BALLADS

GREAT SONGS
FROM THE IRISH
FOLK TRADITION

EMMA BYRNE

EOIN O'BRIEN

THE O'BRIEN PRESS
DUBLIN

CONTENTS

Introduction 6

CRAIC AND DRINK 9

Are Ye Right There Michael? 11

Finnegan's Wake 17

I'll Tell Me Ma 21

The Irish Rover 25

Lanigan's Ball 31

The Rare Old Mountain Dew 37

The Waxies' Dargle 41

REVOLUTION AND NATIONALISM 45

Arthur McBride 47

Boulavogue 53

Follow Me Up to Carlow 57

Kevin Barry 61

A Nation Once Again 65

The Wearing of the Green 69

LOVE AND TRAGEDY 73

As I Roved Out 75

Danny Boy 79

The Dawning of the Day 83

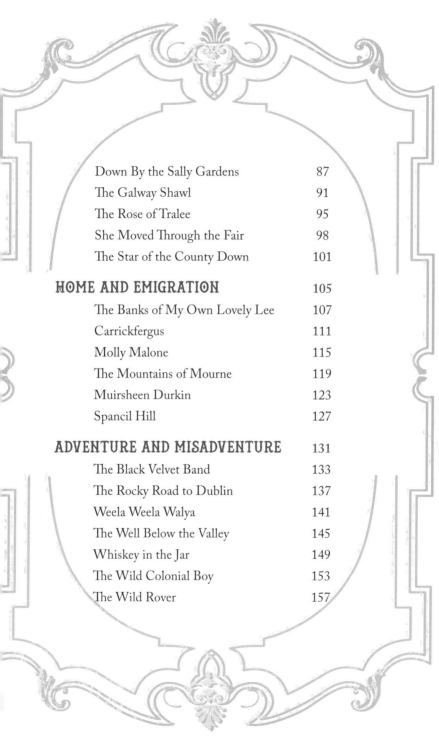

Down By the Sally Gardens 87

The Galway Shawl 91

The Rose of Tralee 95

She Moved Through the Fair 98

The Star of the County Down 101

HOME AND EMIGRATION 105

The Banks of My Own Lovely Lee 107

Carrickfergus 111

Molly Malone 115

The Mountains of Mourne 119

Muirsheen Durkin 123

Spancil Hill 127

ADVENTURE AND MISADVENTURE 131

The Black Velvet Band 133

The Rocky Road to Dublin 137

Weela Weela Walya 141

The Well Below the Valley 145

Whiskey in the Jar 149

The Wild Colonial Boy 153

The Wild Rover 157

INTRODUCTION

Ireland is the only country in the world with a musical instrument as its national symbol. We have an amazing musical heritage, and a big part of this is our ballad tradition. Here you will find songs about tragic love, tragic emigration, tragic uprisings against the British Crown, tragic rovings and ramblings, tragic drinking sessions ... Pretty much every form of tragedy is covered. A very few of the songs are cheerful.

Every county of Ireland has its own county song, and most medium-sized towns and medium-sized landmarks seem to have their own local song too, celebrating the scenery or commemorating some tragically courageous act in the area's history.

For this book, we have picked the cream of the crop of Irish ballads, songs that have stood the test of time, that stir the soul, get the toes tapping and oblige the listener to sing along. They have infectious melodies and evocative lyrics. You don't have to be a great singer to sing these ballads – it's all about the passion you put into it.

There are plenty of familiar characters to be found in these pages: the spurned lover, the sweet and innocent country girl, the brave freedom fighter, the sly recruiting sergeant, the dissolute drunk, the sweet-tongued rogue, all drawn larger than life. Some more surprising figures too: migrant labourers, highwaymen, train drivers, bricklayers, poitín makers, murderers and ghosts.

The origins of many of the songs are unclear, lost in the passing of time and the wanderings of feet. Many were written in the nineteenth century, but some of them go back several hundred more years.

These songs have been passed down orally through generations, and so there are many variations – in the words, in the melodies and in the phrasing. Many have optional extra verses. We have chosen our favourite versions, and in some cases what are presented here are compounds of a few different versions. These songs have been interpreted and accompanied in many different ways, and the chords for backing them are also open to interpretation. Again, we have chosen how we like to hear them.

The woodcuts are reproduced from *Irish Street Ballads,* a collection published in 1939 by Colm Ó Lochlainn's Sign of the Three Candles Press. They had been reproduced in that valuable book from original 'broadsheet' copies of the songs, also printed in Dublin.

It has been an amazing journey, becoming immersed in these songs. Most of them are very familiar, and yet we have discovered clever turns of phrase and lyrical gymnastics, powerful evocations of people and times long gone and yet still living, beautiful melodies and chord structures, subtlety and power. We hope that you will enjoy them as much as we do.

Emma Byrne and Eoin O'Brien, September 2020

CRAIC AND DRINK

The Irish have a reputation for knowing how to have fun, and also a reputation for this usually involving a drink or two. These songs illustrate both of these aspects of the Irish personality. Here we have mayhem at a wake and at a ball, voyages by train and by twenty-seven-masted cargo ship, the joys of poitín making, a Belfast street rhyme and scrounging the price of a pint on the streets of Dublin.

Moyasta Junction, County Clare, one of the stops on the West Clare Railway.

Are Ye Right There Michael?

This was written by Percy French (1854–1920), one of the country's foremost songwriters and entertainers, whose other hits include 'The Mountains of Mourne' and 'Phil the Fluter's Ball'. The song was inspired by an actual train journey French took in 1896, on the famous West Clare Railway service. He left Sligo in the early morning and arrived so late for an eight o'clock recital that the audience had packed up and left.

The song caused huge embarrassment for the railway company, which took a libel case against French. The story goes that French arrived late to the court hearing, and when the judge questioned him on his tardiness, he responded, 'Your honour, I travelled by the West Clare Railway.' The judge duly dismissed the case.

Are Ye Right There Michael?

You may talk of Col-um-bus-'s sail-ing a - cross the At - lan - tic - al Sea, But he nev - er tried to go rail - ing from Enn - is as far as Kil - kee. You run for the train in the mor - nin', the ex - cur - sion train start-in' at eight, You're there when the clock gives a war-nin', But there for an hour you will wait. And as you're wai - ting in the train, you'll hear the guard sing this ref - rain: Are ye right there Mich-ael, are ye right? Do you think that we'll be home be-fore the night? Ah you've been so long in start-in' that you could-n't say for cer-tain, still ye might now Mich - ael, so ye might.

They find out where the engine's been hiding
And it drags you to sweet Corofin.
Says the guard, 'Back her down on the siding,
There's a goods from Kilrush coming in.'
Perhaps it comes in two hours,
Perhaps it breaks down on the way;
If it does, says the guard, be the powers,
We're here for the rest of the day.

And while you sit and curse your luck
The train backs down into a truck:

Are ye right there Michael, are ye right?
Have ye got the parcel there for Mrs White?
Ye haven't, oh begorrah,
Say it's coming down tomorrow,
And it might now Michael, so it might.

At Lahinch, the sea shines like a jewel,
With joy you are ready to shout,
When the stoker cries out, 'There's no fuel
And the fire's tee-totally out,
But hand up that bit of a log there
I'll soon have ye out of the fix.
There's a fine clamp of turf in the bog there,
And the rest go a-gathering sticks.'

And while you're breaking bits of trees
You hear some wise remarks like these:

Are ye right there Michael, are ye right?
Do ye think that you can get the fire to light?
Oh, an hour you'll require,
For the turf it might be drier;
Well it might now Michael, so it might.

Kilkee! You may never get near it.
You're in luck if the train brings you back,
For the permanent way is so queer
It spends most of its time off the track.
Uphill the old engine is climbing
While the passengers push with a will;
You're in luck when you reach Ennistymon,
For all the way home is downhill.

And as you're wobbling through the dark
You hear the guard make this remark:

Are ye right there Michael, are ye right?
Do you think that we'll be there before it's light?
It all depends on whether
The old engine holds together,
And it might now Michael, so it might, so it might,
And it might now Michael, so it might.

Uisce beatha, the water of life.

Finnegan's Wake

This is the story of Tim Finnegan, a builder's labourer, who, being fond of a drop of the hard stuff, falls off a ladder, breaks his skull and is assumed to be dead.

As he is waked, the mourners get carried away with drinking, dancing and fighting. Some whiskey gets splashed on the corpse, whereupon Finnegan miraculously comes back to life and joins in the celebrations of his own death. Whiskey – *uisce beatha*, 'the water of life' – has caused both Finnegan's death and his subsequent resurrection.

This comic masterpiece famously provided the title for James Joyce's last and most impenetrable work, *Finnegans Wake*, published in 1939. Tim Finnegan's comic resurrection becomes a symbol of the universal cycle of life, very much a theme of the book.

'Finnegan's Wake' may have been written in the 1860s in a New York Irish ghetto. It was famously sung and recorded by The Clancy Brothers and Tommy Makem, as well as by The Dubliners.

Finnegan's Wake

Tim Fin-ne-gan lived in Wal-kin Street, a gen - tle Ir-ish-man, migh-ty odd, He
had a brogue both rich and sweet, and to rise in the world he car-ried a hod. Ah but
Tim had a bit of a tipp-lin' way, with a love of liq-our he was born, And to
send him on his way each day he'd a drop of the cray-thur eve - ry morn.
Whack fol the da now, dance to your part-ner, A - round the floor your trot-ters shake,
Was-n't it the truth I told you? Lots of fun at Finn-eg-an's wake.

One morning Tim was rather full,
His head felt heavy, which made him shake.
He fell from the ladder and he broke his skull
And they carried him home his corpse to wake.
They rolled him up in a nice clean sheet
And laid him out upon the bed,
With a gallon of whiskey at his feet
And a barrel of porter at his head.

Whack fol the da, now ...

18

His friends assembled at the wake
And Mrs Finnegan called for lunch.
First they brought in tay and cake,
Then pipes, tobacco and whiskey punch.
Biddy O'Brien began to cry,
'Such a nice clean corpse did you ever see?
Tim Mavourneen, why did you die?'
'Arrah hold your gob,' said Paddy McGee.

Whack fol the da, now ...

Then Maggie O'Connor took up the job,
'O Biddy,' says she, 'you're wrong, I'm sure.'
Biddy gave her a belt in the gob
And left her sprawling on the floor.
Then the war did soon engage,
It was woman to woman and man to man,
Shillelagh law was all the rage
And a row and a ruction soon began.

Whack fol the da, now ...

Then Mickey Maloney raised his head
When a bucket of whiskey flew at him,
It missed and, falling on the bed,
The liquor scattered over Tim.
Tim revives, see how he rises,
Timothy rising from the bed,
Said, 'Whirl your whiskey around like blazes,
Thundering Jesus, do you think I'm dead?'

Whack fol the da, now ...

City Hall, Belfast.

I'll Tell Me Ma

This children's folk song was collected in Britain in the nineteenth century. The chorus mentions Belfast, but it has also been adapted to Dublin.

The song is coupled with a children's game. Children make a ring by joining hands and one player stands in the centre. If the child in the centre is a girl, she is asked, 'Please won't you tell me who is he?' and she gives the initials of a boy in the ring. If it's a boy in the centre, he gives a girl's initials. The children in the ring sing the rest of the words and the person who had their initials called goes into the centre.

A notable recording was made in 1988 by Van Morrison and The Chieftains, on *Irish Heartbeat*. Ronnie Drew of The Dubliners also recorded it with The Chieftains. Sham Rock's 1998 version reached number thirteen in the UK singles chart, selling over 200,000 copies. There are other versions by The Clancy Brothers and Tommy Makem, The Dubliners and Sinéad O'Connor.

I'll Tell Me Ma

Albert Mooney says he loves her.
All the boys are fighting for her.
They knock at the door and ring at the bell,
Sayin', 'Oh my true love, are you well?'
Out she comes as white as snow,
Rings on her fingers and bells on her toes.
Ole Jenny Murray says she'll die
If she doesn't get the fella with the roving eye.

I'll tell me ma ...

Let the wind and the rain and the hail blow high
And the snow come tumbling from the sky.
She's as nice as apple pie,
She'll get her own lad by and by.
When she gets a lad of her own,
She won't tell her ma when she gets home.
Let them all come as they will,
For it's Albert Mooney she loves still.

I'll tell me ma ...

Cobh, County Cork.

The Irish Rover

Attributed to songwriter Joseph M Crofts, and most recently made famous by The Pogues and Ronnie Drew, this song features a monstrous ship 'with twenty-seven masts', a mad crew and a huge cargo. The ship goes on a fantastical voyage from Cork to New York.

As the song goes on, the verses grow more exuberant. The famous cargo reads like the contents of a witch's cauldron, and includes bricks, bales of old billy goats' tails, buckets of stones, blind horses' hides, barrels of bones, hogs, dogs, barrels of porter, and Sligo rags. The seven-year voyage ends in disaster when the vessel sinks. The captain's dog is finally drowned and only the narrator survives, as the 'last of the *Irish Rover*'.

It has also been recorded by Dominic Behan, The Clancy Brothers and Tommy Makem.

The Irish Rover

We had one million bags of the best Sligo rags,
We had two million buckets of stones,
We had three million sides of old blind horses' hides,
We had four million barrels of bones,
We had five million hogs, had six million dogs,
Seven million barrels of porter,
We had eight million bales of old nanny goats' tails
In the hold of the *Irish Rover*.

There was old Mickey Coote who played hard on his flute
When the ladies lined up for his set.
He was tootin' with skill for each sparkling quadrille,
Though the dancers were fluther'd and bet.
With his sparse witty talk he was cock of the walk
And he rolled the dames under and over,
They all knew at a glance when he took up his stance
And he sailed in the *Irish Rover*.

There was Barney McGee from the banks of the Lee,
There was Hogan from County Tyrone,
There was Jimmy McGurk, who was scared stiff of work
And a man from Westmeath called Malone,
There was Slugger O'Toole, who was drunk as a rule
And fighting Bill Tracey from Dover
And your man Mick McCann from the banks of the Bann
Was the skipper of the *Irish Rover*.

For a sailor it's always a bother in life,
It's so lonesome by night and by day,
'Til he launch for the shore and this charming young whore,
Who will melt all his troubles away.
All the noise and the rout, swillin' poitín and stout,
For him soon the torment's over.
Of the love of a maid, he's never afraid,
An old sot from the *Irish Rover*.

We had sailed seven years when the measles broke out,
And the ship lost its way in a fog,
And that whale of a crew was reduced down to two,
Just meself and the captain's old dog.
Then the ship struck a rock, oh Lord, what a shock.
The bulkhead was turned right over,
Turned nine times around, and the poor old dog was drowned.
I'm the last of the *Irish Rover*.

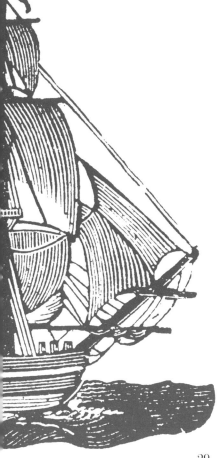

Reflections on the water in Athy, County Kildare.

Lanigan's Ball

Possibly written by DK Gavan with music by John Candy, or by Tony Pastor with music by Neil Bryant, this song has been around since the 1860s, and probably longer. Some sources say it was previously known as 'Harry the Jug'.

It tells the tale of one Jeremy Lanigan of Athy, County Kildare. He inherits a farm on the death of his father, and decides to throw a massive shindig to thank all the friends and relations who helped him when times were hard. There is enormous work involved in preparing for the ball, including the narrator's dancing lessons in Dublin. The lyrics go on to describe the partygoers, and the food and drink consumed. Inevitably, a fight eventually breaks out and puts an end to Lanigan's ball.

Well-known recordings include those by The Bards, Christy Moore and the Dropkick Murphys, who changed the title to 'Flannigan's Ball'. Frank Kelly parodied it with 'Charlie Stepped In', lampooning the Arms Trial of 1970.

Lanigan's Ball

Myself, to be sure, I got free invitations
For all the nice girls and boys I might ask,
In less than a minute both friends and relations
Were dancing as merry as bees round a cask.
Lashings of punch and wine for the ladies,
Potatoes and cakes, there was bacon and tea.
There were the Nolans, Dolans, O'Gradys,
Courting the girls and dancing away.

Six long months I spent in Dublin ...

They were doing all kinds of nonsensical polkas,
Round the room in a whirly gig,
But Julia and I soon banished their nonsense
And tipped them a twist of a real Irish jig.
Oh, how the girls they really got mad at me,
Dancing till you'd think the ceiling would fall,
For I spent six months at Brook's Academy
Learning to dance for Lanigan's ball.

Six long months I spent in Dublin ...

The boys were as merry, the girls all hearty,
Dancing around in couples and groups,
Till an accident happened, young Terence McCarthy
He put his right leg through Miss Finnerty's hoops.
The creature she fainted and cried 'holy murder!'
And called for her brothers and gathered them all.
Carmody swore that he'd go no further
Till he'd satisfaction at Lanigan's ball.

Six long months I spent in Dublin ...

Boys, oh boys, 'tis then there was ructions,
Myself got a kick from big Phelim McHugh,
And I soon replied to his kind introduction
And kicked up a terrible hullabaloo.
Casey the piper was near getting strangled,
They squeezed up his pipes, bellows, chanters and all,
And the girls in their ribbons they all got entangled
And that put an end to Lanigan's ball.

Six long months I spent in Dublin ...

The Rare Old Mountain Dew

The 'rare old mountain dew' is, of course, poitín, Ireland's traditional illicit spirit, named after the small pot stills it was made in, which could be dismantled and hidden easily. In 1661, the English King Charles II introduced the first excise tax on alcohol, creating the divide between legal 'parliament whiskey' and illegal poitín or poteen. In the eighteenth and nineteenth centuries, running battles between 'revenue men' and distillers were not uncommon.

The song, extolling the miraculous virtues of this traditional beverage, was written for a play called *The Blackbird*, produced in Dublin in 1882, with lyrics by Edward Harrigan, set to an older tune. The earliest recording was in 1927 by John Griffin, under the title 'The Girl I left Behind'.

The chorus is a piece of lilting, or diddling, a way of carrying a tune traditionally used to accompany dancers when no instruments were at hand.

In The Pogues' famous song 'Fairytale of New York', an old man poignantly sings 'The Rare Old Mountain Dew' as he declares that his days are numbered.

The Rare Old Mountain Dew

Let gras-ses grow and riv-ers flow in a free and ea-sy way, Just
give me en-ough of the rare old stuff that's made near Gal-way Bay. And
p'lice-men all from Do-ne-gal, Sli-go and Lei-trim too, We'll
give them the slip when we take a sip of the rare old moun-tain dew. Hi the
did-dle-y I dil-lum, did-dle-y doo-dle I dil-lum, did-dle-y doo-ri did-dle-y di day, Hi the
did-dle-y I dil-lum, did-dle-y doo-dle I dil-lum, did-dle-y doo-ri did-dle-y di day.

At the foot of the hill there's a neat little still,
Where the smoke curls up to the sky.
By the smoke and the smell you can plainly tell
That there's poitín brewin' nearby,
For it fills the air with a perfume rare,
And betwixt both me and you,
As home we stroll, we can take a bowl
Or a bucket of the mountain dew.

Hi the diddley I dillum ...

Now learned men who use the pen
Have sung the praises high
Of the rare poitín from Ireland green,
Distilled from wheat and rye.
Put away your pills, it'll cure all ills,
Be ye pagan, Christian or Jew,
So take off your coat and grease your throat
With the dear old mountain dew.

Hi the diddley I dillum ...

St Patrick's Church in Ringsend, Irishtown, a short distance outside the medieval city walls of Dublin.

The Waxies' Dargle

Shoemakers and menders were known in Dublin as waxies, after the waterproof waxed thread they used. The Dargle is a river in County Wicklow; well-to-do Dubliners went there for picnics, and its name became synonymous with a day out.

The waxies, unlike the gentry, didn't get as far as Wicklow, but their regular outings to the seafront at Irishtown, near Dublin's docks, became known as the Waxies' Dargle. The original Waxies' Dargle may have been part of Donnybrook Fair, the notorious fair that was closed down in 1855 because of 'riotous behaviour'.

In the Aeolus episode of *Ulysses* by James Joyce, Myles Crawford refers to two old ladies at the top of Nelson's Pillar being out for the 'waxies dargle'.

As well as the famous Galway races, first held in 1869, the song mentions 'Monto' – the area around Montgomery Street, a famous red-light district in the centre of Dublin, immortalised as 'Nighttown' in *Ulysses* – and Capel Street, which was renowned for pawnbroking shops.

The Waxies' Dargle

Says my aul' wan to your aul' wan, 'Will you go to the Wax-ies' Dar-gle?' Says

your aul' wan to my aul' wan, 'Sure I hav-en't got a far - thing.'

I went up to Mon - to town, to see Un-cle Mc - Ar - dle, But he

would-n't give me half a crown for to go to the Wax-ies' Dar - gle.

'What will you have?' 'I'll have a pint, I'll have a pint with you, sir. And if

one of you does-n't or - der soon we'll be chucked out of the boo - zer.

42

Says my aul' wan to your aul' wan,
'Will ye go to the Galway races?'
Says your aul' wan to my aul' wan,
'I'll hawk me aul' man's braces.
I went up to Capel Street
To the Jewish moneylenders,
But he wouldn't give me a couple of bob
For the aul' man's red suspenders.'

'What will you have?' ...

Says my aul' wan to your aul' wan,
'We've got no beef or mutton.
If we went up to Monto town
We might get a drink for nuttin'.'
Here's a nice piece of advice
I got from an aul' fishmonger:
'When food is scarce and you see the hearse,
You'll know you've died of hunger.'

'What will you have?' ...

Statue of a pikeman at Ballinamuck, County Longford.

REVOLUTION AND NATIONALISM

Hundreds of years of occupation and oppression by the British Empire gave the Irish plenty of time to write revolutionary songs. There are songs marking every rising and revolt, and songs from all the years between these events. Though some of them are hundreds of years old, there is still tremendous power in them, as they express a deep yearning for freedom and independence.

Killybegs, County Donegal.

Arthur McBride

Set during the Napoleonic wars era (c. 1803–15), this song begins with the narrator and his cousin Arthur innocently out walking by the sea on Christmas morning. They are approached by a recruiting sergeant, a corporal and a 'little wee drummer', who try to induce the men to join the British Army, telling them how great a soldier's life is, and what nice clothes soldiers get to wear. McBride replies that the sergeant's clothes belong to the army, and he and his cousin have no interest in going to war.

The sergeant takes offence, and threatens the heroes, whereupon they hit the soldiers over the heads with their shillelaghs. Not content with this, they throw the soldiers' swords and the drummer's drum into the sea, and beat the soldiers to a pulp.

This song was collected in 1840 by Patrick Joyce, and also by George Petrie in Donegal, where it is thought to originate, McBride being a common Donegal name. It has been recorded by several artists, including Planxty, Christy Moore and Bob Dylan. Ours is a simplified version of Paul Brady's masterful recording.

Arthur McBride

'Good morning! Good morning!' the sergeant did cry,
'And the same to you, gentlemen!' we did reply,
Intending no harm, meaning just to pass by,
For it being on Christmas morning.
But says he, 'My fine fellows, if you will enlist,
It's ten guineas of gold I will place in your fist
And a crown in the bargain for to kick up the dust
And drink the King's health in the morning.

'For a soldier he leads a very fine life
And he always is blessed with a charming young wife.
He pays all his debts without quarrel or strife
And always lives pleasant and charming.
And a soldier he always is decent and clean,
In the finest of clothing he's constantly seen,
While other poor fellows go dirty and mean
And sup on thin gruel in the morning.'

'But,' says Arthur, 'I wouldn't be proud of your clothes,
For you've only the lend of them, as I suppose,
And you dare not change them one day, for you know
If you do you'll be flogged in the morning.
And although that we are single and free,
we take great delight in our own company
And we have no desire strange places to see,
Although that your offer is charming.

'And we have no desire to take your advance,
All hazards and dangers we barter on chance,
For you would have no scruples for to send us to France,
Where we could get shot without warning.'

'Now!' said the sergeant, 'I'll have no such chat,
And I neither will take it from spalpeen or brat,
For if you insult me with one further word
I'll cut off your heads in the morning.'

And with that, me and Arthur, we soon drew our hods
And we scarce gave them time for to draw their own blades,
When a trusty shillelagh came over their heads
And bade them take that as fair warning.
And their own rusty rapiers that hung by their side,
We flung them as far as we could in the tide.
'Now take them out, devils!' cried Arthur McBride,
'And temper their edge in the morning.'

And the little wee drummer we flattened his pow,
And we made a football of his rowdeydowdow,
Threw it in the tide for to rock and to row
And bade it a tedious returning.
And we having no money, paid them off in cracks,
And we paid no respect to their two bloodied backs,
But lathered them there like a pair of wet sacks
And left them for dead in the morning.

And so to conclude and to finish disputes
We obligingly asked if they wanted recruits,
For we were the lads who would give them hard clouts
And bid them look sharp in the morning.
Oh, me and my cousin, one Arthur McBride,
As we went a-walkin' down by the seaside,
Now mark what followed and what did betide,
For it being on Christmas morning.

Monument to
Father John Murphy,
Enniscorthy, County Wexford.

Boulavogue

'Boulavogue' was composed by Patrick Joseph McCall, who also wrote 'Kelly the Boy from Killane' and 'Follow Me Up To Carlow'. Written for the centenary of the 1798 Rebellion, the song was first printed in the *Irish Independent* on 18 June 1898, entitled 'Fr Murphy of the County of Wexford'. It has become something of an anthem for Wexford.

'Boulavogue' commemorates the campaign of Father John Murphy and his army in County Wexford in 1798. Father Murphy, a local priest, at first tried to persuade people not to take part in the Rebellion, but he became a reluctant rebel leader after soldiers burned down his parishioners' homes.

The Wexford insurgents fought bravely against professional troops, routing the British cavalry at Oulart Hill and raiding the garrison at Enniscorthy. They were eventually defeated at the Battle of Vinegar Hill on 21 June 1798. Although evading capture that day, Father Murphy and other leaders were tracked down, tortured and hanged.

Notable recordings of 'Boulavogue' include versions by Brian Roebuck, The Dubliners, The Clancy Brothers and Tommy Makem, Irish tenor Anthony Kearns, ballad group The Flying Column and recently The High Kings.

Boulavogue

At Bou - la - vogue as the sun was set-ting O'er the bright May mea - dows of Shel - ma - lier, A reb - el hand set the hea - ther blaz-ing, And brought the neigh - bours from far and near. Then Fath - er Mur-phy from old Kil - cor - mack Spurred up the rock with a war - ning cry, Arm, arm, he cried, for I've come to lead you, For Ire - land's free - dom we'll fight or die.

He led us on against the coming soldiers,
The cowardly yeomen we put to fight,
'Twas at the harrow, the boys of Wexford
Showed Bookie's regiment how men could fight.
Look out for hirelings, King George of England,
Search every kingdom where breathes a slave,
For Father Murphy from the County Wexford
Sweeps o'er the land like a mighty wave.

We took Camolin and Enniscorthy,
And Wexford storming, drove out our foes;
'Twas at Slieve Coillte our pikes were reeking
With the crimson stream of the beaten yeos.
At Tubberneering and Ballyellis
Full many a Hessian lay in his gore.
Ah, Father Murphy, had aid come over,
The green flag floated from shore to shore.

At Vinegar Hill o'er the pleasant Slaney,
Our heroes vainly stood back to back.
And the yeos of Tullow took Father Murphy
And burned his body upon the rack.
God grant you glory, brave Father Murphy,
And open Heaven to all your men,
For the cause that called you may call tomorrow,
In another fight for the green again.

A cottage at the base of a waterfall in Glenmalure, County Wicklow.

Follow Me Up to Carlow

This song commemorates the Battle of Glenmalure on 25 August 1580, when Fiach Mac Hugh O'Byrne, 'the firebrand of the mountains', defeated 3,000 English soldiers in the Second Desmond Rebellion. An Irish Catholic force led by O'Byrne and James FitzEustace, Viscount Baltinglass, defeated the English force led by Baron Arthur Grey de Wilton, at the O'Byrne stronghold of Glenmalure in the Wicklow Mountains.

Grey had come to Ireland to put down the Rebellion and protect the Pale, the area around Dublin. Against the advice of veteran commanders, he led his army through Kildare into the Wicklow Mountains, where they were ambushed by O'Byrne.

Reputed to have been played as the soldiers marched into battle, the air is a very warlike march. The equally blood-stirring words were written by Patrick Joseph McCall, and appear in his 1899 collection *Songs of Erinn*, under the title 'Marching Song of Feagh McHugh'.

Notable recordings of the song are by Planxty and The Wolfe Tones. A Polish version of the song ('Do Carlow') was recorded by the band Mordewind.

Follow Me Up to Carlow

See the swords of Glen Imayle flashing o'er the English Pale,
See all the children of the Gael beneath O'Byrne's banners.
Rooster of a fighting stock, would you let a Saxon cock
Crow out upon an Irish rock? Fly up and teach him manners.

Curse and swear, Lord Kildare ...

From Tassagart to Clonmore, there flows a stream of Saxon gore.
O, great is Rory Óg O'More at sending loons to Hades.
White is sick and Lane is fled, now for black Fitzwilliam's head.
We'll send it over dripping red to Queen Liza and the ladies.

Curse and swear, Lord Kildare ...

Mountjoy Prison, Dublin.

Kevin Barry

A well-known and much loved Irish rebel song, this ballad commemorates Kevin Barry, an IRA Volunteer who was hanged by the British during the War of Independence, aged eighteen. His execution helped to inflame public opinion against British rule.

Having joined the IRA in 1917, aged fifteen, Barry took part in several arms raids. On the morning of 20 September 1920, his unit was to ambush a British Army truck on Bolton Street in Dublin and seize weapons, after which he would return to University College Dublin, where he was a medical student, to sit an exam. The British soldiers surrendered to the IRA men, but a shot was fired by somebody and, in the confusion, three soldiers were killed. Barry's unit fled, but he was captured and sentenced to death. There was an international campaign for clemency, with many pointing out that captured British soldiers, as prisoners of war, were not executed by the IRA. However, the execution went ahead on 1 November 1920.

Well-known performances are by The Wolfe Tones and The Clancy Brothers. Paul Robeson and Leonard Cohen also sang the song.

Kevin Barry

In Mount-joy Jail, one Mon-day mor - ning, high up - on the gall-ows tree, Kev-in

Bar - ry gave his young life for the cause of li-ber - ty. But a

lad of eigh-teen sum - mers, still there's no - one can de - ny, As he

walked to death that mor - ning he proud-ly held his head up high.

Just before he faced the hangman, in his dreary prison cell,
The Black and Tans tortured Barry, just because he wouldn't tell
The names of his brave comrades, and other things they wished to know.
'Turn informer and we'll free you.' Kevin Barry answered, 'No.'

'Shoot me like a soldier. Do not hang me like a dog,
For I fought to free old Ireland on that still September morn,
All around the little bakery where we fought them hand to hand.
Shoot me like a brave soldier, for I fought for Ireland.'

'Kevin Barry, do not leave us. On the scaffold you must die!'
Cried his broken-hearted mother as she bade her son goodbye.
Kevin turned to her in silence, saying, 'Mother, do not weep,
For it's all for dear old Ireland, and it's all for freedom's sake.'

Calmly standing to attention while he bade his last farewell
To his broken-hearted mother, whose grief no one can tell.
For the cause he proudly cherished this sad parting had to be,
Then to death walked softly smiling, that old Ireland might be free.

Another martyr for old Ireland; another murder for the Crown,
Whose brutal laws to crush the Irish could not keep their spirit down.
Lads like Barry are no cowards, from the foe they will not fly.
Lads like Barry will free Ireland. For her sake they'll live and die.

Children of Lir
sculpture at
Dublin's Garden
of Remembrance, by
Oisín Kelly.

A Nation Once Again

Thomas Osborne Davis (1814–45), a founder of the nationalist Young Ireland organisation, felt that music could have a powerful impact on the mood of the people. This song, written by Davis, was first published in *The Nation* on 13 July 1844, and it became a rallying cry for the Irish republican movement.

The narrator dreams of a time of freedom, and exhorts the Irish people to fight for their lands: 'And righteous men must make our land a nation once again.' As rebel songs go, nothing says it plainer.

Famous recordings include those by John McCormack, The Clancy Brothers, The Dubliners and, most famously, The Wolfe Tones. In 2002, after an email campaign, The Wolfe Tones' version was voted the world's most popular song, according to the BBC World Service global poll of listeners. It came in just ahead of a patriotic Hindi song, 'Vande Mataram'.

A Nation Once Again

When boy-hood's fire was in my blood, I read of an-cient free men. For Greece and Rome, who brave - ly stood, three hun-dred men and three men, And then I prayed I yet might see our fet - ters rent in twain, And Ire - land, long a pro - vince, be a nat - ion once a - gain. A nat - ion once a - gain, a nat - ion once a - gain, And Ire - land, long a pro - vince, be a nat - ion once a - gain.

And from that time, through wildest woe, that hope has shone
    a far light,
Nor could love's brightest summer glow outshine that solemn
    starlight;
It seemed to watch above my head, in forum, field and fane.
Its angel voice sang round my bed, a nation once again.

A nation once again ...

It whisper'd too that freedom's ark and service high and holy
Would be profaned by feelings dark and passions vain or lowly,
For freedom comes from God's right hand and needs a godly
    train,
And righteous men must make our land a nation once again.

A nation once again ...

So, as I grew from boy to man, I bent me to that bidding.
My spirit of each selfish plan and cruel passion ridding,
For thus I hoped some day to aid – oh, can such hope be vain?
When my dear country shall be made a nation once again!

A nation once again ...

Green shamrock is a strong symbol of Ireland.

The Wearing of the Green

This ballad laments the suppression of supporters of the 1798 Rebellion. It has an old Irish air and there are many versions of the lyrics, but the best known is by the Irish actor and playright Dion Boucicault (1820–90), based on a Dublin street ballad.

The Society of United Irishmen, inspired by the ideas of the American and French revolutions, was the main force behind the Rebellion. It was made up of Presbyterians, angry at being shut out of power by the Anglican establishment, and Catholics, who made up the majority of the population. They adopted green as their colour, and supporters wore green-coloured garments or ribbons, or a sprig of shamrock.

Their cause was helped by a French army that landed in Mayo, but ultimately it failed, with a death toll of between 10,000 and 30,000. The leader of the Rebellion, Theobald Wolfe Tone (1763–98), a Protestant, was sentenced to be hanged on 10 November 1798, but he died the previous night of a neck wound – it is unclear whether it was suicide or murder.

Famous recordings include those by John McCormack, Judy Garland and The Wolfe Tones.

The Wearing of the Green

Then since the colour we must wear is England's cruel red,
Sure Ireland's sons will ne'er forget the blood that they have shed.
You may take the shamrock from your hat and cast it on the sod,
But 'twill take root and flourish there, though under foot it's trod.
When the law can stop the blades of green from growing as they grow,
And when the leaves in summertime their verdure dare not show,
Then I will change the colour that I wear in my canteen;
But 'til that day, please God, I'll stick to wearing of the green.

Oh the wearing of the green ...

LOVE AND TRAGEDY

Ireland's ballad tradition includes some of the
world's most famous love songs. Most of them
have tragic endings, as lovers are torn from each
other by emigration, death, jealousy, pride or just
circumstances. Some are simpler celebrations
of love and beauty.

The ruins of a famine cottage in County Donegal.

As I Roved Out

The theme of 'As I Roved Out' is found in numerous Irish songs – a soldier, a sailor or a nobleman spies a beautiful young maiden whilst out roving the country, and charms his way into her bed. Inevitably she is abandoned in the end; sometimes it is because he is married, sometimes because he loves another. In this case, the hero marries another because she owns some land.

This song is thought to be allegorical, and dates back to the days of the famine, when any bit of property was enough to tempt a man to jilt his true love in favour of the lassie with the land.

'As I Roved Out' features a sinuous, ever-changing melody that seems to hover above the chords, always searching for resolution. Great performances include those by Planxty, with Andy Irvine accompanying himself on hurdy-gurdy, The Voice Squad's harmony a capella version, and a soulful rendition by Dungiven's Cara Dillon.

As I Roved Out

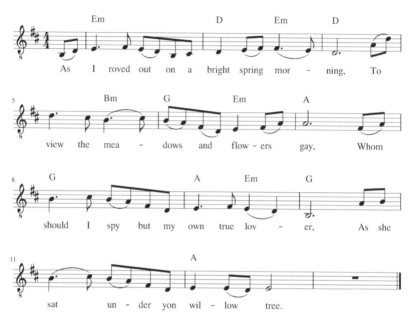

As I roved out on a bright spring mor - ning, To
view the mea - dows and flow - ers gay, Whom
should I spy but my own true lov - er, As she
sat un - der yon wil - low tree.

I took off my hat and I did salute her,
I did salute her most courageously.
When she turned around, well the tears fell from her,
Sayin', 'False young man, you have deluded me.

'A diamond ring I owned I gave you,
A diamond ring to wear on your right hand,
But the vows you made, love, you went and broke them
And married the lassie that had the land.'

'If I married the lassie that had the land, my love,
It's that I'll rue until the day I die.
When misfortune falls, sure no man can shun it.
I was blindfolded, I'll ne'er deny.'

Now at night when I go to my bed of slumber,
The thoughts of my true love run in my mind.
When I turn around to embrace my darling,
Instead of gold, sure it's brass I find.

And I wish the Queen would call home her army
From the West Indies, Amerikay and Spain,
And every man to his wedded woman,
In hopes that you and I will meet again.

Cushendall in the Glens of Antrim.

Danny Boy

Probably the most famous Irish ballad of them all, 'Danny Boy' was written by Frederic Weatherly in 1913, set to the tune of the 'Derry Air', an ancient Irish melody published in 1796.

Many have interpreted the song as a message from a parent to a son who is going off to war, or leaving home. Certainly it has become an unofficial signature song for Irish-Americans and Irish-Canadians in particular, but also for all the global Irish. There was a huge surge in its popularity in the 1920s among the Irish diaspora in America. The song was played at Elvis Presley's funeral and at services for victims of 9/11.

Artists who have recorded it include Judy Garland, Bing Crosby, Johnny Cash, Jackie Wilson, Elvis Presley and Andrea Bocelli. So popular is this song that in 2008, Foley's pub in New York banned its playing for the month of March!

Danny Boy

Oh Dan-ny boy, the pipes, the pipes are call-ing, From glen to glen, and down the moun-tain side. The sum-mer's gone and all the leaves are fall-ing, 'Tis you, 'tis you must go and I must bide. But come you back when sum-mer's in the mead-ow, And all the Val-ley's hushed and white with snow, And I'll be here in sun-shine or in sha-dow, Oh Dan-ny boy, oh Dan-ny boy, I love you so.

But when ye come, and all the flowers are dying,
If I am dead, as dead I well may be,
You'll come and find the place where I am lying
And kneel and say an Ave there for me.

And I shall hear, though soft you tread above me,
And o'er my grave will warmer, sweeter be,
For you will bend and tell me that you love me,
And I shall sleep in peace until you come to me.

Statue of the poet Patrick Kavanagh by
John Coll, situated on the north bank of
the Grand Canal on Mespil Road, Dublin.

The Dawning
of the Day

The original Irish-language version of this song, entitled 'Fáinne Geal an Lae' (literally 'the bright ring of the day'), was published in 1847's *Irish Popular Songs*. 'Fáinne Geal an Lae' is an *aisling*, or traditional love song, in which the narrator meets a mysterious and beautiful woman, who then leaves him as the dawn approaches.

The air is based on a tune from the seventeenth century, probably composed by Thomas Connellan. The simpler, nineteenth-century air is one of the first tunes taught to aspiring tin whistle players.

But the melody is doubtlessly better known as the setting for 'Raglan Road', whose lyrics are a poem by Patrick Kavanagh. In this song, the poet meets a beautiful woman on Raglan Road, in south Dublin. He knows that the relationship will end tragically, yet he can't help continuing 'along the enchanted way'.

'The Dawning of the Day' was beautifully sung by Count John McCormack from Athlone, County Westmeath, legendary for his astonishing breath control.

The Dawning of the Day

One mor - ning ear - ly as I walked forth By the
mar - gin of Lough Leinn, The
sun - shine dressed the trees in green And the
sum - mer bloomed a - gain. I
left the town and wan - dered on Through
fields all green and gay, And who
should I meet but my col - leen bawn At the
daw - ning of the day.

No cap or cloak this maiden wore,
Her neck and feet were bare.
Down to the grass in ringlets fell
Her glossy golden hair.
A milking pail was in her hand,
She was lovely, young and gay.
Her beauty excelled even Helen of Troy
At the dawning of the day.

On a mossy bank I sat me down
With the maiden by my side.
With gentle words I courted her
And asked her to be my bride.
She said, 'Young man, don't bring me blame,
But let me go away,
For the morning light is shining bright
At the dawning of the day.'

Goat willow, also known as the pussy willow or great sallow, is a common species of willow, native to Europe.

Down By the Sally Gardens

This well-known poem by William Butler Yeats, which was published in the collection *The Wanderings of Oisín and Other Poems*, was set to music by Herbert Hughes in 1909, to the traditional air 'The Moorlough Shore' or 'The Maids of Mourne Shore'.

The first verse comes from a recollection that Yeats had of a song sung by an old woman in Ballisodare, County Sligo, and in fact Yeats originally called his poem 'An Old Song Re-Sung'. The song he heard might have been 'The Rambling Boys of Pleasure', which has one very similar verse.

It has been suggested that the location of the 'Sally Gardens' is along the banks of the Ballisodare River, where people harvested reeds for thatching. A 'sally', or *saileach*, is a willow rod.

Many artists have recorded this song, including John McCormack, Marianne Faithfull, Tommy Makem and Liam Clancy, and Dolores Keane.

Down By the Sally Gardens

In a field down by the river, my love and I did stand,
And on my drooping shoulder, she placed her snow-white hand.
She bid me take life easy, as the grass grows on the weirs,
But I was young and foolish, and now am full of tears.

Two women wearing traditional shawls return
from Mass on Inis Meáin, the Aran Islands.

The Galway Shawl

This traditional folk-song is full of suppressed passion and emotion. The narrator meets a beautiful woman, and they clearly get along very well. She invites him to her home, and he plays several traditional tunes to her father, as she sings along. Her father is noted as being 'six feet tall', the clear implication being that the narrator must be on his best behaviour. Though he has to leave and go home to Donegal, he can't stop thinking about the woman, and tears fill her eyes at his departure.

The song is set in Oranmore, County Galway, and was first collected in 1936 by Sam Henry, sung by Bridget Kealey from Dungiven, County Derry. Sam Henry himself was a man of many parts, including customs officer, antiquarian, writer, photographer, folklorist and musician.

Famous recordings include those by The Dubliners, and Vinnie Jones on *The X Factor*!

The Galway Shawl

In Or - an - more   in the Coun - ty Gal - way,   One plea - sant
eve - ning   in the month of May,   I spied a
dam - sel,   she was young and hand - some,   Her beau - ty
fair - ly   took my breath a - way.

She wore no jewels, nor costly diamonds,
No paint nor powder, no none at all,
But she wore a bonnet with ribbons on it
And 'round her shoulders was the Galway shawl.

We kept on walking, she kept on talking,
Till her father's cottage came into view.
Said she, 'Come in, sir, and meet my father
And play, to please him, "The Foggy Dew".'

She sat me down beside the hearthstone.
I could see her father; he was six feet tall.
And soon her mother had the kettle singing.
All I could think of was the Galway shawl.

She wore no jewels …

I played 'The Black Bird', 'The Stack of Barley',
'Rodney's Glory' and 'The Foggy Dew'.
She sang each note like an Irish linnet,
And tears welled in her eyes of blue.

'Twas early, early, all in the morning,
I hit the road for old Donegal.
Said she, 'Goodbye, sir.' She cried and kissed me,
But my heart remains with the Galway shawl.

She wore no jewels …

The Roses out on parade for the first time on the Denny Street stage at The Rose of Tralee International Festival, August 2012 in Tralee, County Kerry.

The Rose of Tralee

This ballad is so famous, it has inspired an international festival, held annually in Tralee, County Kerry, at the end of August. Written in the nineteenth century, the words are credited to Edward Mordaunt Spencer and the tune to Charles William Glover.

However, it is said in Tralee that the song was written by the wealthy William Pembroke Mulchinock, who fell in love with Mary Pauline O'Connor, a maid in service to his family. Because of the class difference, the romance was frowned upon. He went abroad for a time; upon his return, he found that Mary had died.

The song is strongly associated with the Irish diaspora. It has featured in many movies, as well as albums, and has been sung by actors Denis O'Dea, Gordon MacRae and Jimmy O'Brien, as well as Bing Crosby, John McCormack and many more.

The song was used by the Irish rugby team at the 1987 World Cup, instead of a national anthem. Tom Waits sang about dancing with the Rose of Tralee in his song 'Rain Dogs', after Waits and his wife Kathleen spent their honeymoon in Tralee.

The Rose of Tralee

The cool shades of evening their mantels were spreading,
And Mary all smiling was listening to me.
The moon through the valley her pale rays was spreading
When I won the heart of the rose of Tralee.

She was lovely and fair ...

She Moved Through the Fair

The narrator here is looking forward to his wedding – his prospective in-laws don't mind his lack of 'kine', or cattle. He watches as his lover moves away from him through the fair, having told him that 'it will not be long, love, 'til our wedding day'. How she comes to her end isn't specified, but she returns to him as a ghost, repeating the same words, suggesting perhaps their imminent reunion in the afterlife.

The melody is in Mixolydian mode – in a major key, but with a minor seventh note – giving it a haunting and ethereal sound. It was first collected in Donegal by poet Pádraig Colum and musicologist Herbert Hughes. There are many variants of the song, in some of which the spouse-to-be runs off with another man.

English folk group Fairport Convention recorded the song in 1968, and Art Garfunkel recorded a version in 1977. The song 'Belfast Child' by Simple Minds incorporates the melody. A spine-tingling version by Sinéad O'Connor was used in the film *Michael Collins*.

She Moved Through the Fair

And she stepped away from me and moved through the fair,
And fondly I watched her move here and move there,
And then she went homeward, with one star awake,
Like the swan in the evening moves over the lake.

Last night she came to me, my dead love came in.
So softly she entered, her feet made no din,
And she laid her hand on me, and this she did say:
'It will not be long, love, 'til our wedding day.'

The River Bann at the Agivey Bridge,
County Antrim.

The Star of the County Down

Set near Banbridge, County Down, this tells of a young man who meets a charming young woman called Rose McCann, the 'star of the County Down'. During their brief encounter, he becomes infatuated with her, taken in particular by her 'nut-brown' hair and her singing and dancing skills. He resolves to dress in his finest clothes, hoping to meet her at the harvest fair and win her heart.

The melody was also used in an Irish folk-song called 'My Love Nell', and the words were written by Cathal McGarvey (1866–1927). Each line has an internal rhyme, as well as rhyming at the end.

Well-known people who have recorded this song include Van Morrison, The Pogues and Canadian singer Loreena McKennitt. Israeli singer Ehud Banai recorded a version in Hebrew, which translates as 'The Star of Gush Dan District'.

The Star of the County Down

Near to Ban-bridge town in the Coun-ty Down one mor-ning in Ju-ly, Down a
bo-reen green came a sweet col-leen and she smiled as she passed me by, Oh she
looked so neat, from her two bare feet to the sheen of her nut-brown hair, Such a
coax-ing elf, sure I shook my-self for to see I was real-ly there. From
Ban-try Bay up to Der-ry Quay and from Gal-way to Dub-lin town, No
maid I've seen like the sweet col-leen that I met in the Coun-ty Down.

As she onward sped I shook my head and I gazed with a feeling queer
And I said, says I, to a passerby, 'Who's your one with the nut-brown hair?'
He smiled at me, and with pride says he, 'She's the gem of old Ireland's crown.
Young Rosie McCann from the banks of the Bann, and the star of the
    County Down.'

From Bantry Bay up to Derry Quay ...

She'd a soft brown eye and a look so sly and a smile like the rose in June,
And you held each note from her auburn throat as she lilted lamenting tunes.
At the pattern dance you'd be in a trance as she skipped through a jig or reel,
When her eyes she'd roll, as she'd lift your soul and your heart she would
    likely steal.

From Bantry Bay up to Derry Quay ...

At the harvest fair she'll be surely there, and I'll dress in my Sunday clothes,
With my hat cocked right and my shoes shone bright, for a smile from the
    nut-brown Rose.
No horse I'll yoke, or pipe I'll smoke, till the rust in my plough turns brown
And a smiling bride by my own fireside sits the star of the County Down.

From Bantry Bay up to Derry Quay ...

HOME AND EMIGRATION

Ireland has a long history of emigration, most
notably around the mid-nineteenth century, when
the population collapsed from over eight million
to just over four million. There are many beautiful
songs on the subject of an emigrant's yearning for
the place of his birth, often eulogising the scenery
and particularly the womenfolk to be found there.
Those who managed to stay at home have also
celebrated Ireland's wonders in song.

Patrick's Bridge over the River Lee in Cork city.

The Banks of
My Own Lovely Lee

There is probably nobody on Earth prouder of where they come from than the people of Cork. Written by Dick Forbes and JC Flanahan (or possibly Shanahan), this song is often referred to as the 'Cork anthem', and it is unabashed in its celebration of the scenery thereabouts.

The words, set to a suitably elaborate melody, share the author's love of his hometown, from his childhood days through to adulthood – the beauty of the countryside, and special moments spent there with friends and loved ones.

The River Lee rises in the Shehy Mountains, near Gougane Barra on the west Cork border, and flows eastward towards Cork city, where it splits in two, creating an island on which the city centre is built. The Mardyke, mentioned in the first verse, is an area of Cork city historically left as an open space. In 1791, city clerk Edward Webber drained and landscaped the area. He constructed a promenade and teahouse, and the fashionable area was called the Meer Dyke Walk, after the Meer Dyke in Amsterdam.

The Banks of My Own Lovely Lee

How oft do my thoughts in their fan - cy take flight to the
home of my child - hood a - way, To the
days when each pat - ri - ot's vis - ion seemed bright 'ere I
dreamed that those joys should de - cay, When my
heart was as light as the wild winds that blow down the
Mar - dyke through each elm tree, Where I
sport - ed and played 'neath each green leaf - y shade on the

1. banks of my own love - ly Lee, Where I

2. banks of my own love - ly Lee.

And then in the springtime of laughter and song,
Can I ever forget the sweet hours?
With the friends of my youth as we rambled along
'Mongst the green mossy banks and wild flowers.
And then, when the evening sun, sinking to rest,
Sheds its golden light over the sea,
The maid with her lover the wild daisies pressed
On the banks of my own lovely Lee.
The maid with her lover the wild daisies pressed
On the banks of my own lovely Lee.

'Tis a beautiful land this dear isle of song;
Its gems shed their light to the world.
And her faithful sons bore thro' ages of wrong
The standard Saint Patrick unfurled.
Oh! Would I were there with the friends I love best
And my fond bosom's partner with me,
We'd roam thy banks over, and when weary we'd rest
By thy waters, my own lovely Lee.
We'd roam thy banks over, and when weary we'd rest
By thy waters, my own lovely Lee.

Oh, what joys should be mine ere this life should decline
To seek shells on thy sea-girdled shore,
While the steel-feathered eagle, oft splashing the brine,
Brings longing for freedom once more.
Oh, all that on Earth I wish for or crave
Is that my last crimson drop be for thee,
To moisten the grass of my forefathers' grave
On the banks of my own lovely Lee.
To moisten the grass of my forefathers' grave
On the banks of my own lovely Lee.

Carrickfergus Castle, County Antrim.

Carrickfergus

Named after the town on Belfast Lough in County Antrim, the song 'Carrickfergus' is mostly set in Kilkenny. 'Ballygran', mentioned in the song, could very well be the local Ballingarry coalmines.

Collector George Petrie obtained two settings of the melody from Patrick Joyce, also a collector. Petrie believed that the air to which it was set, 'Do Bhí Bean Uasal', was a Munster song in origin. The Irish-language version of the song is about a man being cuckolded, and is bawdy and humorous, while the English version is more sentimental.

It was first recorded in 1965 as 'The Kerry Boatman' by Dominic Behan. The Clancy Brothers also recorded a version. It has been recorded by many international performers, and was played at the 1999 funeral of John F Kennedy Junior, while Russian singer-songwriter Aleksandr Karpov translated the lyrics into Russian. It is very similar to the song 'The Water is Wide', recorded by Bob Dylan, Pete Seeger and Bryan Ferry.

Carrickfergus

My childhood days bring back sad reflections
Of happy times we spent so long ago.
My boyhood friends and my own relations
Have all passed on now like melting snow.
So I spend my days in ceaseless roving,
Soft is the grass and my bed is free.
Oh, to be home now in Carrickfergus
On the long winding road down to the sea.

Now in Kilkenny it is reported
On marble stones there as black as ink.
With gold and silver I would support her,
But I'll sing no more now till I get a drink,
'Cause I'm drunk today, and I'm seldom sober,
A handsome rover from town to town.
Ah, but I'm sick now, my days are numbered.
Come all ye young men and lay me down.

Statue of Molly Malone, Suffolk Street, Dublin.

Molly Malone

Probably the most popular Dublin folk-song of all time, 'Molly Malone' remains an unofficial anthem of the city. It has a music-hall, rather than folk, feel to it, similar to 'My Darling Clementine'.

There is a little convincing evidence that Molly, the fishmonger who plied her trade on the streets of Dublin, was a real person. However, in 1988, the Dublin Millennium Commission endorsed claims for a Mary Malone who died on 13 June 1699, and 13 June is now Molly Malone Day.

Molly has her own statue, created by Jeanne Rynhart and unveiled in 1988. It was originally placed at the bottom of Grafton Street, but in 2014 moved to the less-busy Suffolk Street. The bronze on her famous bust has been worn to a shine by 'handsy' tourists. The statue is known colloquially as The Tart With the Cart, or The Trollop With the Scallops, as there is a suggestion that Molly was a fishmonger by day and a prostitute by night.

U2, Danny Kaye, Pete Seeger and Johnny Logan have all recorded the song, as have The Dubliners and Sinéad O'Connor. Welsh bass-baritone Bryn Terfel recorded an operatic version.

Molly Malone

In Dub-lin's fair ci-ty, Where the girls are so pre-tty, I first set my eyes on sweet Mo-lly Mal-one, As she wheeled her wheel-bar-row Through streets broad and nar-row, Cry-ing, 'Cock-les and muss-els, a - live a-live oh.' A-live a-live oh, a - live a-live oh, Cry-ing, 'Cock-les and muss-els, a - live a-live oh.'

She was a fishmonger,
And sure, 'twas no wonder,
For so were her mother and father before,
And they both wheeled their barrows
Through streets broad and narrow,
Crying, 'Cockles and mussels, alive alive oh.'

Alive alive oh ...

She died of a fever
And sure, no one could save her
And that was the end of sweet Molly Malone;
Now her ghost wheels her barrow
Through streets broad and narrow,
Crying, 'Cockles and mussels, alive alive oh.'

Alive alive oh ...

The Mourne Mountains photographed from Murlough Beach.

The Mountains of Mourne

This is another Percy French classic, with music composed by Houston Collisson. The melody may be based on the folk tune 'Carrigdonn', the tune that Thomas Moore used for his song 'Bendemeer's Stream'. Brendan O'Dowda and Finbar Furey have recorded it, as has Don McClean.

'The Mountains of Mourne' tells the story of an emigrant from a village near the Mourne Mountains in County Down who has travelled to London for work. Although fascinated by the busy lifestyle and fashions he sees there, he is all the time missing his true love back home.

The dramatic Mourne Mountains include the highest point in Northern Ireland, Slieve Donard, at 850 metres. The name derives from a Gaelic clan who lived there, the Múghdorna.

The First World War song, 'Old Gallipoli's A Wonderful Place', borrows the melody and some phrases from 'The Mountains of Mourne'. The Battle of Gallipoli in 1916 was a costly defeat for the Allies by the Ottoman Empire.

The Mountains of Mourne

I believe that when writing a wish you expressed
As to how the fine ladies of London were dressed,
But if you'll believe me, when asked to a ball,
They don't wear no tops to their dresses at all.
Oh, I've seen them myself and you could not in truth
Tell if they were bound for a ball or a bath.
Don't be startin' them fashions now, Mary Machree,
Where the Mountains of Mourne sweep down to the sea.

There's beautiful girls here, oh, never you mind,
Beautiful shapes nature never designed,
Lovely complexions of roses and cream,
But let me remark with regard to the same
That if at those roses you venture to sip
The colours might all come away on your lip,
So I'll wait for the wild rose that's waiting for me
In the place where the dark Mourne sweeps down to the sea.

You remember young Peter O'Laughlin, of course,
But he's over here with the rest of the force.
I saw him one day as he stood on the strand,
And he stopped the whole street with one wave of his hand.
And as we were talking of days that are gone,
The whole population of London looked on,
But for all his great powers, he's wishful like me
To be back where the dark Mourne sweeps down to the sea.

Famine cottage ruins on the Dingle Peninsula, County Kerry.

Muirsheen Durkin

Another great song of emigration and the diaspora, this tells the story of a man off to prospect for gold in the California Gold Rush. Unusually, it is an optimistic emigration song – the protagonist is leaving behind digging 'praties' (potatoes) and expects soon to be digging lumps of gold.

It is sung to the air of '*Cailíní deasa Mhuigheo*', or 'Pretty Girls of Mayo', a popular reel from the nineteenth century. 'Muirsheen' is probably a phonetic approximation of the name Mairtín, or Martin.

News broke in 1848 of gold being found in California, and it brought 300,000 people to the west coast from the rest of the United States and around the world. It had terrible effects on the native people there, as whole indigenous societies were attacked and pushed off their lands by the gold-seekers, known as 'forty-niners' after the year 1849, the peak year of the rush.

Well-known performers of this song include Christy Moore, Sharon Shannon, The Pogues, Johnny McEvoy and The Dubliners.

Muirsheen Durkin

Goodbye Muirsheen Durkin, I'm sick and tired of workin'.
No more I'll dig the praties and no longer I'll be fooled.
As sure as me name is Carney, I'll be off to Californy,
Instead of diggin' praties I'll be diggin' lumps of gold.

I've courted girls in Blarney, in Kanturk and in Killarney,
In Passage and in Queenstown that is the Cobh of Cork,
But I'm tired of all this pleasure so I'm off to take my leisure,
And the next time that you hear from me I'll write you from New York.

Goodbye Muirsheen Durkin ...

Goodbye to all the girls at home, I'm going far across the foam
To try and make me fortune in far Americay.
There's gold and jewels in plenty for the poor and for the gentry,
And when I return again I never more will say

Goodbye Muirsheen Durkin ...

Spancil Hill Horse
Fair takes place
annually on 23 June.

Spancil Hill

Michael Considine, who wrote this song, was born at Spancil Hill, near Ennis in County Clare, around 1850, and emigrated to the US around 1870. At that time, in the wake of the famine, there was huge emigration from the area. It is a song of yearning for the familiar people and places of his youth, and Considine hoped to make enough money to pay for Mary MacNamara, the girl mentioned in the last two verses, to join him.

Spancil Hill Horse Fair is one of the oldest in the country, held annually on 23 June. The name Spancil Hill may come from the practice of 'spancilling', hobbling an animal by tying the left foreleg to the right hind leg with a short rope, to stop the animal from moving away.

The lyrics below are the best-known version of this song, as sung both by The Dubliners and by Christy Moore; the original is considerably longer.

Michael Considine worked in Boston for two years before moving to California. He wrote the poem and sent it home to his nephew, but he never saw his homeland again.

Spancil Hill

Last night as I lay dream - ing of pleas - ant days gone by, My

mind being bent on ram - bl - ing, to Ire - land I did fly. I

stepped on board a vi - sion and foll - owed with a will, Till at

last I came to an - chor at the cross near Span - cil Hill.

It being the twenty-third of June, the day before the fair,
When lreland's sons and daughters in crowds assembled there,
The young and the old, the brave and the bold, their journey to
  fulfil.
There were jovial conversations at the fair of Spancil Hill.

I went to see my neighbours to hear what they might say.
The old ones were all dead and gone, the young ones turning
  grey.
I met with tailor Quigley, he's as bould as ever still.
Sure he used to make my britches when I lived in Spancil Hill.

I paid a flying visit to my first and only love.
She's as white as any lily and as gentle as a dove.
She threw her arms around me, saying, 'Johnny, I love you still.'
Oh, she's Ned the farmer's daughter and the flower of Spancil
  Hill.

I dreamed I held and kissed her, as in the days of yore.
She said, 'Johnny you're only joking, like many's the time
  before.'
The cock crew in the morning, he crew both loud and shrill
And I awoke in California, many miles from Spancil Hill.

The Tasman Monument with a statue of Abel Tasman at Salamanca Place, Hobart, Tasmania, Australia.

SYRUP

ADVENTURE AND MISADVENTURE

This section features a poor innocent framed by a beautiful woman and sentenced to transportation to Tasmania; a young man in search of work, walking across Ireland and winding up in Liverpool, lamenting his station in life; dark tales of infanticide and incest in remote, rural places; a highwayman tricked by a conniving lover; an emigrant from Kerry who becomes a sort of Australian Robin Hood; and finally a young man with a reputation for drinking and trouble who comes home to redeem his name.

Statue of Luke Kelly,
sculpted by John Coll, in
King Street, Dublin.

Luke Kelly
1940 - 1984
'Dubliner'

Sculptor / Dealbhadóir John Coll 2019

The Black Velvet Band

This is the tragic story of a young Belfast apprentice who is beguiled by a beautiful woman. She steals a watch from a passing gentleman's pocket, and then plants it on his person. Arrested, he appears in court the next day and is sentenced to seven years' penal servitude in Van Diemen's Land, or Tasmania. The narrator ends with a warning to all young men, to 'beware of the pretty colleens'. In some versions, the 'roguish' woman's motivation is made clear – she has met a new beau and wants to be rid of the young apprentice.

'The Black Velvet Band' was first published as a broadsheet by Swindells of Manchester, sometime between 1796 and 1853, and later by H Such of London, between 1863 and 1885. The song has been collected in Britain, Ireland and Australia. A staple of the Irish ballad repertoire, the best-known version is probably the 1967 recording by The Dubliners, with Luke Kelly's powerful voice belting out the tune.

The Black Velvet Band

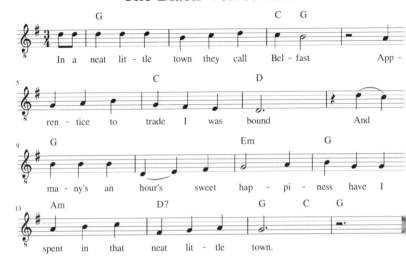

In a neat lit - tle town they call Bel - fast App -
ren - tice to trade I was bound And
ma - ny's an hour's sweet hap - pi - ness have I
spent in that neat lit - tle town.

A sad misfortune came over me,
Which caused me to stray from the land,
Far away from me friends and relations,
Betrayed by the black velvet band.

Her eyes they shone like diamonds,
I thought her the queen of the land,
And her hair, it hung over her shoulder,
Tied up with a black velvet band.

I took a stroll down Broadway,
Meaning not long for to stay,
When who should I meet but this pretty fair maid
Come a-traipsing along the highway.

She was both fair and handsome,
Her neck, it was just like a swan,
And her hair, it hung over her shoulder,
Tied up with a black velvet band.

Her eyes they shone like diamonds ...

I took a stroll with this pretty fair maid,
And a gentleman passing us by,
Well, I knew she meant the doing of him,
By the look in her roguish black eye.

A gold watch she took from his pocket
And placed it right into my hand,
And the very first thing that I knew was
I'd landed in Van Diemen's Land.

Her eyes they shone like diamonds ...

Before the judge and the jury
Next morning, I had to appear.
The judge, he says to me,
'Young man, you're case it is proven clear.

'We'll give you seven years' penal servitude
To be spent far away from the land,
Far away from your friends and relations,
Betrayed by the black velvet band.'

Her eyes they shone like diamonds ...

So come all you jolly young fellows,
A warning take by me,
When you are out on the town, me lads,
Beware of the pretty colleens.

They'll feed you with strong drink, me lads,
'Til you are unable to stand,
And the very next thing that you'll know is
You've landed in Van Diemen's Land.

Her eyes they shone like diamonds ...

The Liffey pub in Liverpool, which has the
strongest Irish heritage of any British city.

The Rocky Road to Dublin

Written by 'the Galway Poet' DK Gavan for English music-hall performer Harry Clifton in the mid-nineteenth century, this is the story of a green young man leaving his home in Tuam, County Galway, in search of work.

He begins well, but then he is robbed, mocked repeatedly, placed with some pigs in the hold of a ship, suffers severe sea sickness and finally gets into a fight in Liverpool. Outnumbered, he is rescued by some men from his home county. There are many variations to the lyrics, and the original version had two extra verses. Bits of the song are recited by Mr Deasy in James Joyce's *Ulysses*.

The 9/8, or 'slip jig', rhythm gives the song great momentum, with a bar of 12/8 in the last line of the verse just to mix things up. Well-known recordings include those by The Rolling Stones, The Clancy Brothers and Tommy Makem, The Dubliners, Bert Jansch, Christy Moore, Damian Dempsey and Johnny Logan.

The Rocky Road to Dublin

While in the mer-ry month of June, Now from me home I star-ted, Left the girls of Tu-am
near - ly bro-ken hear-ted, Sa - lut - ed fath - er dear, Kissed me dar - lin' moth - er,
Drank a pint of beer, Me grief and tears to smoth-er, Then off to reap the corn and
leave where I was born, Cut a stout black-thorn to ban - ish ghosts and go - b - lins, A
brand new pair of brogues, to rat - tle o - ver the bogs, And frigh - ten all the dogs,
On the roc - ky road to Du-b-lin, One, two, three, four, five, Hunt the hare and turn her,
Down the roc - ky road and all the way to Du-b-lin, Whack fol-lol de dah.

In Mullingar that night I rested limbs so weary,
Started by daylight next morning bright and early,
Took a drop of pure to keep me heart from shrinking;
That's the Paddy's cure when'er he's on for drinking.
To hear the lassies smile, laughing all the while
At me curious style, 'twould set your heart a-bubblin'.
They asked me was I hired, the wages I required,
'Til I was almost tired of the rocky road to Dublin.

One, two, three four, five …

In Dublin next arrived, I thought it such a pity
To be so soon deprived a view of that fine city,
So then I took a stroll, all among the quality,
Bundle it was stolen, in a neat locality.
Something crossed me mind, when I looked behind
No bundle could I find upon me stick a-wobblin'.
Enquiring for the rogue, said me Connacht brogue
Wasn't much in vogue on the rocky road to Dublin.

One, two, three four, five …

From there I got away, me spirits never failing,
Landed on the quay just as the ship was sailing.
Captain at me roared, said that no room had he;
When I jumped aboard, a cabin found for Paddy
Down among the pigs; I played some funny rigs,
Danced some hearty jigs, the water round me bubblin'.
When off Holyhead I wished meself was dead,
Or better far instead, on the rocky road to Dublin.

One, two, three four, five …

The boys of Liverpool, when we safely landed,
Called meself a fool, I could no longer stand it,
Blood began to boil, temper I was losing,
Poor old Erin's Isle they began abusing.
'Hurrah me soul,' says I, shillelagh I let fly,
Galway boys were by and saw I was a hobblin',
With a loud hurray they joined in the affray,
We quickly cleared the way for the rocky road to Dublin.

One, two, three four, five …

Weela Weela Walya

This rather sinister schoolyard song, on the theme of infanticide, emerged during the harsh period of the famine of 1845–49, a time of mass starvation and disease in Ireland. An estimated one million people died, and another million emigrated. Stories have emerged from the time of mothers killing their children because they couldn't feed them. But 'weile waile' or 'weilewei' was a much earlier expression of grief and despair, words associated with weeping and wailing, going back to the middle ages.

The song was collected by folklorist Francis James Child and included in his 1898 anthology, *Child's Ballads*. It was popularised by Irish folk bands The Dubliners and The Clancy Brothers in the 1960s, and was sung at the funeral of Ronnie Drew in 2008. Similar murder ballads, 'The Cruel Mother' and 'Old Mother Lee', have been collected in England.

It is suggested that the River Salya, or Sáile, could be the Rover Poddle, a tributary of the Liffey in south Dublin.

Weela Weela Walya

There was an old wom-an and she lived in the woods, wee - la wee - la wal - ya, There was an old wom-an and she lived in the woods, down by the riv - er Sal - ya.

She had a baby three months old,
Weela weela walya ...

She had a pen-knife long and sharp,
Weela weela walya ...

She stuck the pen-knife in the baby's heart,
Weela weela walya ...

Two policemen and a Special Branch man,
Weela weela walya ...

They put a rope around her neck,
Weela weela walya ...

They pulled the rope and she got hung,
Weela weela walya ...

And that was the end of the woman in the wood,
Weela weela walya ...

St Patrick's Well at Struell, County Down.

The Well Below the Valley

This is another sinister murder ballad, dealing not only with multiple deaths but also with incest. The lily, of course, represents death.

Also known as 'The Maid and the Palmer', it combines themes from the Bible, including the stories of the Samaritan woman and Mary Magdalene. A gentleman, or a pilgrim or *palmer*, asks for a drink from a maid at a well. He says that if her lover came, she would give him a drink. She replies that she has no lover, but he tells her she has borne six babies, fathered by her uncle, her brother and her father, and he tells her where she has buried them. She asks what will happen to her and is told she will be transformed into a bell clapper for seven years, and then spend seven years in Hell.

The song is traditionally popular in the Traveller community. Probably the best-known recording is by Planxty on the album *The Well Below the Valley*, but it has also been performed by Christy Moore.

The Well Below the Valley

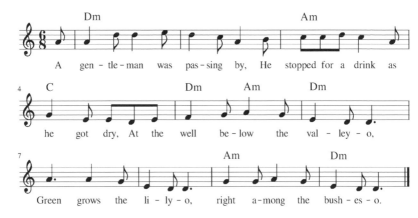

A gen - tle - man was pas - sing by, He stopped for a drink as
he got dry, At the well be - low the val - ley - o,
Green grows the li - ly - o, right a - mong the bush - es - o.

My cup is full up to the brim,
If I were to stoop I might fall in
At the well below the valley-o ...

If your true love was passing by
You'd fill him a drink if he was dry
At the well below the valley-o ...

She swore by grass, she swore by corn,
Her true love had never been born
At the well below the valley-o ...

He said to her you're swearing wrong,
Six fine children you've had born
At the well below the valley-o ...

If you be a man of noble fame
You'll tell to me the father of them
At the well below the valley-o ...

There's two of them by your uncle Dan
At the well below the valley-o ...

Two of them by your brother John
At the well below the valley-o ...

Two of them by your father dear
At the well below the valley-o ...

If you be a man of noble fame
You'll tell to me what did happen to them
At the well below the valley-o ...

There's two buried neath the stable door
At the well below the valley-o ...

Another two by the kitchen door
At the well below the valley-o ...

Another two buried beneath the well
At the well below the valley-o ...

If you be a man of noble fame
You'll tell to me what will happen myself
At the well below the valley-o ...

You'll be seven years a-ringing a bell
At the well below the valley-o ...

And seven more a-portin' in Hell
At the well below the valley-o ...

I'll be seven years a-ringing a bell
But the Lord above may save my soul
From portin' in Hell
At the well below the valley-o ...

147

Carrauntoohil, the tallest peak in Ireland,
Macgillycuddy's Reeks, County Kerry.

Whiskey in the Jar

This is the tale of a highwayman in the southwest of Ireland, who waylays and robs a British army officer. Ultimately he is betrayed by his lover, and ends up in prison. Elements of the song are similar to the earlier 'Patrick Flemmen He Was a Valiant Soldier', about Patrick Fleming, an Irish highwayman executed in 1650.

In the seventeenth century, bandits who harassed British landlords and soldiers were regarded as folk heroes of a sort, like England's Robin Hood. They were known as tories (from *tóraidhe*, raider) or rapparees. Famous Irish highwaymen included James Freney, who operated around Kilkenny, Count Redmond O'Hanlon from Armagh, Jeremiah Grant of Tipperary and Willy Brennan, hanged in Cork in 1804 and immortalised in the song 'Brennan on the Moor'.

While it was a signature song of The Dubliners in the 1960s, Thin Lizzy's hard rock interpretation from 1972 is probably the best-known version. It has also been performed by the Grateful Dead and Metallica, who won a Grammy award for their heavy rock version.

Whiskey in the Jar

I counted out his money and it made a pretty penny,
I put it in my pocket and I took it home to Jenny.
She swore that she would love me, never would she leave me,
But the devil take that woman, for you know she fooled me easy.

Musha ring dum a doo dum a dah ...

I went up to my chamber, all for to take a slumber,
I dreamed of gold and jewels and for sure it was no wonder,
But Jenny blew my charges and she filled them up with water,
Then sent for Captain Farrell to be ready for the slaughter.

Musha ring dum a doo dum a dah ...

'Twas early in the morning, just before I rose to travel,
Up comes a band of footmen and likewise Captain Farrell.
I first produced my pistol for she stole away my rapier.
I couldn't shoot the water, so a prisoner I was taken.

Musha ring dum a doo dum a dah ...

There's some take delight in the carriages a-rolling
And others take delight in the hurling and the bowling,
But I take delight in the juice of the barley
and courting pretty fair maids in the morning bright and early.

Musha ring dum a doo dum a dah ...

If anyone can aid me 'tis my brother in the army,
If I can find his station in Cork or in Killarney,
And if he'll go with me, we'll go rovin' through Kilkenny,
And I'm sure he'll treat me better than my own a-sporting Jenny.

Musha ring dum a doo dum a dah ...

Looking towards Castlemaine Harbour,
Dingle Peninsula, County Kerry.

The Wild Colonial Boy

This song was originally about Jack Donahue, a nineteenth-century Irish rebel and convict who became a bushranger. Things didn't end well for him, as he was eventually shot by the police. The song was banned, as it painted bushrangers in a bad light.

The colonial boy was renamed as Jack Duggan, an emigrant who left Castlemaine, County Kerry, for Australia, in the years after the famine. Another popular highwayman, he robbed from the rich to feed the poor. In an Australian version, the hero hails from Castlemaine in Australia's Victoria province.

It has been recorded by The Clancy Brothers, Dr Hook, Burl Ives and Oliver Reed, and featured in the movie *The Quiet Man*. Mick Jagger sings it in the 1970 movie *Ned Kelly*, about the real-life outlaw of the same name, best known for wearing a suit of bulletproof armour during his last shootout with the police.

The Wild Colonial Boy

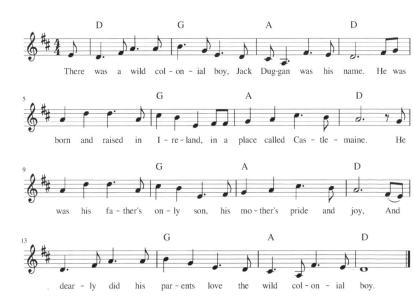

There was a wild col - on - ial boy, Jack Dug-gan was his name. He was

born and raised in I - re - land, in a place called Cas - tle - maine. He

was his fa - ther's on - ly son, his mo - ther's pride and joy, And

dear - ly did his par - ents love the wild col - on - ial boy.

At the early age of sixteen years, he left his native home,
And to Australia's sunny shore he was inclined to roam.
He robbed the rich, he helped the poor, he shot James McAvoy;
A terror to Australia was the wild colonial boy.

One morning on the prairie as Jack he rode along,
A-listening to the mockingbird a-singing a cheerful song,
Out stepped a band of troopers, Kelly, Davis and Fitzroy;
They all set out to capture him, the wild colonial boy.

'Surrender now, Jack Duggan, for you see we're three to one.
Surrender in the Queen's high name, for you're a plundering son.'
Jack pulled two pistols from his belt and he proudly waved them high;
'I'll fight, but not surrender,' said the wild colonial boy.

He fired a shot at Kelly, which brought him to the ground,
And turning round to Davis, he received a fatal wound;
A bullet pierced his proud young heart from the pistol of Fitzroy;
And that was how they captured him, the wild colonial boy.

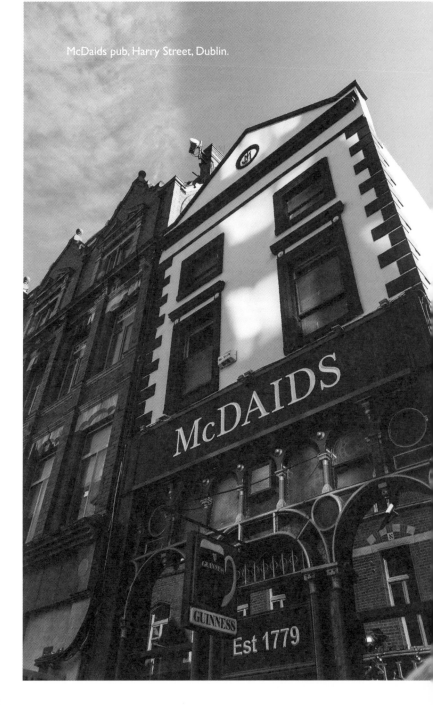

McDaids pub, Harry Street, Dublin.

The Wild Rover

Although 'The Wild Rover' is a classic pub song to roar along to, it is really about a reformed character returning home, having given up his wild ways and made his fortune abroad.

When the narrator sets foot in a pub, he pretends to be penniless and the landlady refuses him credit. When he takes some gold coins out of his pocket, her attitude changes. He now intends to go home, ask his parents' pardon for previous misdeeds, and settle down.

The song's origins remain largely unknown, but it seems to date from the late sixteenth century. There are possibly hundreds of different versions.

Fans of Glasgow's Celtic Football Club sing the song at away matches. There have been numerous recordings, including by The Dubliners, The Wolfe Tones, The Clancy Brothers, Foster and Allen, Stiff Little Fingers and even André Rieu! Lankum give it a very different treatment on 2019's *The Livelong Day*.

The Wild Rover

I went into an alehouse I used to frequent
And I told the landlady me money was spent.
I asked her for credit, she answered me, 'Nay,
Such a custom as yours I can get any day.'

And it's no, nay, never ...

I then took from my pocket ten sovereigns bright,
And the landlady's eyes opened wide with delight.
She says, 'I have whiskeys and wines of the best,
And the words that you told me were only in jest.'

And it's no, nay, never ...

I'll go home to my parents, confess what I've done,
And I'll ask them to pardon their prodigal son,
And when they've caressed me, as oft' times before,
I never will play the wild rover no more.

Emma Byrne is an artist and designer living in a cottage in rural County Wexford. She grew up listening to the songs in this book.

Eoin O'Brien is a songwriter and musician, a writer and illustrator. He enjoys nothing more than a good old singsong around a kitchen table or a bonfire. He lives with his fantastic wife, two beautiful children and a dog, in historic Glasnevin in north Dublin.